Border Collie Dogs as Pets

The Handy Guide for Border Collies

Border Collie General Info, Purchasing, Care, Keeping, Health, Supplies, Food, and More Included!

By: Lolly Brown

Copyrights and Trademarks

All rights reserved. No part of this book may be reproduced or transformed in any form or by any means, graphic, electronic, or mechanical, including photocopying, recording, taping, or by any information storage retrieval system, without the written permission of the author.

This publication is Copyright ©2019 NRB Publishing, an imprint. Nevada. All products, graphics, publications, software and services mentioned and recommended in this publication are protected by trademarks. In such instance, all trademarks & copyright belong to the respective owners. For information consult www.NRBpublishing.com

Disclaimer and Legal Notice

This product is not legal, medical, or accounting advice and should not be interpreted in that manner. You need to do your own due-diligence to determine if the content of this product is right for you. While every attempt has been made to verify the information shared in this publication, neither the author, neither publisher, nor the affiliates assume any responsibility for errors, omissions or contrary interpretation of the subject matter herein. Any perceived slights to any specific person(s) or organization(s) are purely unintentional.

We have no control over the nature, content and availability of the web sites listed in this book. The inclusion of any web site links does not necessarily imply a recommendation or endorse the views expressed within them. We take no responsibility for, and will not be liable for, the websites being temporarily unavailable or being removed from the internet.

The accuracy and completeness of information provided herein and opinions stated herein are not guaranteed or warranted to produce any particular results, and the advice and strategies, contained herein may not be suitable for every individual. Neither the author nor the publisher shall be liable for any loss incurred as a consequence of the use and application, directly or indirectly, of any information presented in this work. This publication is designed to provide information in regard to the subject matter covered.

Neither the author nor the publisher assume any responsibility for any errors or omissions, nor do they represent or warrant that the ideas, information, actions, plans, suggestions contained in this book is in all cases accurate. It is the reader's responsibility to find advice before putting anything written in this book into practice. The information in this book is not intended to serve as legal, medical, or accounting advice.

Foreword

Border Collie is a sheep – herding canine that have Scottish and English origins. They are one of the best dog breed in the herding family of canines because they are clever, has instinctive abilities, and hardworking.

Many people all over the world keep Collies as pets because aside from their excellent sheep – herding abilities, they usually don't need supervision from their owners when it comes to performing their duties! They can be left to their own devises by with minimal to no supervision, and you can expect them to successfully solve problems and adapt to challenging situations.

As family pets, they are a friendly and loyal breed. You can expect them to still possess that protective instinct by being wary of people they don't know.

If you want to keep a unique, protective, and loyal breed, Border Collies might be the best canine for you! Collies are very intelligent, responsible, hardworking, and a faithful companion, the question is – are you the same? Let's find out!

Table of Contents

Border Collies: Patrolling "Sheep Collisions" Since 1915 1
    A Look Back at History 3
Chapter One: All About the Collies 5
    Breed Standards 6
        Overall Appearance 6
        Coat 7
        Color 8
        Forelegs and Hindlegs 8
        Gait 9
        Head 9
        Neck and Back 10
        Size and Substance 11
    Special Traits of Border Collies 12
    Dealing with Children and Other Household Pets 16
    Competitions 17
Chapter Two: Choosing a Border Collie 19
    Male or Female? 20
        Pros and Cons of Owning a Male Collie 20
        Pros and Cons of Owning a Female Collie 23
    Puppy or Adult? 25
        Pros and Cons of Owning a Collie Puppy 26

Pros and Cons of Owning an Adult 29

Chapter Three: Acquiring a Border Collie 33

The Reputable Breeder Detector 34

Other Sources and Purchase Price 36

Contracts 40

Additional Clauses in the Contract 42

Chapter Four: Bringing Home Your New Border Collie 45

Bringing Home a Border Collie Pup 46

Basic Puppy Supplies 47

Safety Tips 51

Bringing Home an Adult Border Collie 53

Basic Border Collie Supplies 53

Crate Training Your Border Collie 54

Dog – Proofing Your Home 56

Chapter Five: Border Collie's Basic Needs 59

Exercise Needs 60

Factors to Consider When Exercising Your Collie 61

Dangerous Activities 65

Dietary Needs 66

Carnivores or Omnivores? 67

The Diet Switch 67

Wet vs. Dry Food 68

Scheduled Feeding Vs. Free Feeding 69
Home Cooking for Your Border Collie 71
Grooming Needs 73
    Bathing Guidelines 73
    Dental Care 76
    Declawing Your Border Collie 77
Chapter Six: Management of Common Dog Problems 79
    Common Behavioral Problems 80
    Controlling Unnecessary Barking 80
    Jumping Dogs 83
    Biting or Nipping Dogs 86
Chapter Seven: The Aging Dog 91
    Caring for Your Aging Border Collie 92
    Common Health Issues of Senior Dogs 92
    Arthritis and Stiffness 93
    Frequent or Uncontrolled Urination 94
    Blindness and Hearing Loss 94
    Loss of Appetite and Weight Change 95
    Memory Loss 96
Frequently Asked Questions 99
    Glossary of Dog Terms 105
Photo Credits 111

References 113

Border Collies: Patrolling "Sheep Collisions" Since 1915

Yes, you read the title correctly. Border Collies serve as sort of the 'border patrol' when it comes to sheep herding! You can say that they are born leaders because we all know that it's hard to maintain peace and order even for a flock of sheep!

There are various theories about how the dog came to be known as the "Collie." According to historians, the name could have come from 'Coalie' which literally means black, while others think it might have come from a Gaelic word that means "something useful" which is one of the primary characteristic of this breed. On the other hand, most keepers believe that the name simply has Scottish roots since this is where the Collie was originally bred, and they've been known as sheepdogs during early times. In 1915, the Collies became officially known as Border Collie.

Regardless of where the name came from, everyone will agree that Border Collies make an excellent sheep - herding dog, and also a loyal competition dog.

The Border Collie is among the oldest dog breed in the world! They have been at service for many years primarily as a guard dog in both Scotland and England borders. Their ancestors have been known to help farmers and protect large flocks of sheep that dates back to around 36 B.C. according to some history books. We can now assume that patrolling, protecting, and working hard is in their blood! What more can you ask for?

Well, the parent breed of Border Collies also served the Vikings back in the day! Numerous history books tell how the Roman dogs were crossbred with a Spitz – type Viking dog that eventually produced the Border Collie we now know today – more agile, more intelligent, and more hard working than their parent breed combined.

A Look Back at History

In 1873, the very first sheep – dog trial was held in Bala, Wales. The trials are quite similar with the competitions being held today.

In 1906, the first group that officially set the rules for the sheep – dog trial event was formed; it was called the International Sheepdog Trials Society. The same standard set of rules is still being used today. And in 1915, the Secretary of the International Sheepdog Society, James Reid, granted the official name of the breed.

Perhaps the most admirable characteristic of the Collie breed is their desire and love for work. You might see them giving you or other pets the 'eye' while lowering their heads to maintain" peace and order" inside the house, as how they have famously done it with the sheep.

They are very instinctive animals, and they have been known to always know what the sheep will do next which is why you can expect them to be one – step ahead of you! So you better outsmart them – if you can!

They have been known to work independently and under minimal supervision, they have the ability to solve challenging situations with their farmer owners, and they have been use in the livestock industry for a long time.

Today, they have a much better responsibility, and that is to keep you and your family company. They make great guard dogs and they are a loving and loyal pet.

Chapter One: All About the Collies

The Border Collie dogs were bred by shepherd not only because of their strength to work for long hours on the rough terrains of England and Scotland's border but also because of their loyalty and obedience. This kind of selective breeding resulted to a more agile, lean, and intelligent breed that has a unique ability to supervise the sheep.

Back then the main function of the Border Collie was to safely and orderly bring the flock of sheep from the hills down to the rugged terrain of the border, and because their owners recognized their innate ability to herd, the dogs were eventually taught how to drive the stock away, and keep the sheep on a certain area. They have been known to respond to their handler's commands, and they are also quite experts when it comes to 'controlling' a naughty sheep by just using their signature gaze.

Their physical appearance, size, instincts, trainability, obedience, independence, intensity, and energy to work hard are the main reason why it earned the reputation of being perhaps the best herding dog canine.

This chapter will delve on the breed standard of the size as well as their unique behavioral characteristics.

Breed Standards

Overall Appearance

A Border Collie's body structure must have the following traits:

- Medium in size
- Athletic
- Well – balanced and shows soundness, agility, and strength

Chapter One: All About the Collies

- Must have a muscular body structure and the movement must show effortlessness.
- Has keen expression
- Shows stamina
- Shows a tempered manner, unspoiled, alert and must show intelligence

Coat

Border Collies have 2 kinds of coats, but in a competition only one coat may be preferred over the other. Regardless of the coat type, the coats should possess a dense and water – resistant double coats. The top coat should either be straight or wavy while the undercoat should be short and soft.

Smooth Coat

- The body must be smooth with a coarse texture

- Slight feathers on the dog's ruff, forelegs, chest and haunches may also be allowed.

Chapter One: All About the Collies

Rough Coat

- The length of the coat is medium, and should not be excessive

- Has a smooth short coat on the front side of its legs and feet as well as the ears and face.

- Has feathering on the underside, haunches, forelegs and chest.

Color

- If your dog competes, the judges usually accept any kind of color as well as combination of markings as long as white patches aren't too noticeable in the head/ face.

Forelegs and Hindlegs

- The pasterns of the forelegs should be slightly sloped when viewed from the side, and also parallel if it's viewed from the front.

Chapter One: All About the Collies

- A well - muscled shoulder blades that are also equal in length are preferred.
- The forelegs and backlegs must be proportionate to their body.
- The backlegs should also be muscular; the thighs must be long and broad, and it should be sloping to a low set tail.

Gait

- The signature working gaits of the Collie breed are the gallop, and stealth crouch.
- The dog should be able to perform this at a moderate speed.
- The collie should know how to automatically adjust its pace to match the stock that's being worked on.

Head

- The eyes are usually blue but a brown color on one eye is acceptable.

Chapter One: All About the Collies

- Brown – colored eyes with pigmented eye rims are also acceptable.
- The ears must be set well – apart, highly sensitive, and can stand erect/ semi – erect.
- The muzzle should be the same length with the skull which is average in width and relatively flat.
- The under - jaw must be strong and well – developed.
- The nose must have developed nostrils and it should have the same color to the rest of the body.
- The teeth must have a scissors bite.
- The head must have a smart appeal, as well as an alert, obedient and eager look.

Neck and Back

- Their neck must be strong, muscular, and slightly arched.

Chapter One: All About the Collies

- The neck should also be proportionate to the rest of the body.

- The back should be level if viewed from the loins to their withers

- Must have a slightly broad chest

- The tail must NOT be curled otherwise it's a minus point.

Size and Substance

Here are the following sizes and proportions should you choose to enter your Border Collie in a competition:

- The height of withers in females: are 18 inches to 21 inches.

- The height of withers in males: are 19 inches to 22 inches.

- There should be no excess body weight

- The bone must be light and medium in size.

Chapter One: All About the Collies

- The overall body should be balanced in weight, height, length, and bone size.

- Broken teeth and scars received due to work may be acceptable and not deemed as a fault.

The overall personality of the Border Collie should be clever, active, responsive, affectionate to their owners, and in complete control over their work. They should move swiftly and effortlessly.

Special Traits of Border Collies

The Border Collies are one of the few canine breed that can be easily trained regardless of their age especially if you implement the right training methods. They usually respond to rewards and praises just like most dogs but they are known for taking pleasure whenever they do the job well. This section will cover the best traits of the Collie breed.

Chapter One: All About the Collies

They are natural working dogs

Border Collies are passionate about working and helping their owners even in doing small tasks. Obviously, they don't need to control a flock of sheep or do other chores in the farm since you'll be treating them as family pets - unless of course, you have a flock of sheep to take care of!

They are at their best whenever they feel like they are involved in family activities. You won't have problems training them to behave well even if you already acquired them at a more matured age. As the saying goes, "you can't teach old dog new tricks," well with Border Collies, you can! Positive reinforcement is what works best for them as with most dog breeds. You should never punish your collie in a harsh way if they sometimes become lazy or shy to perform tricks.

The only problem with Border Collies is that some of them are usually shy which is why you need to train them to socialize at an early age so that they can get along well with other people and household pets as they grow. Border Collies respond to hand signals, whistle training, and other dog training methods since they've historically learned to obey their farmer owners in the early times. Once you've

Chapter One: All About the Collies

trained them to get along with people and pets, they'll be comfortable with the family and you'll see how obedient they can become provided that you spend quality training time with them.

They have boundless energy in a non – problematic way

Border Collies are best suited for keepers who also love to exercise or go for a run or walk. Your dog will surely enjoy it whenever you take them on a trip around the neighborhood. The best part is that even if they have boundless energy they are still well - disciplined. Compared to other dog breeds, Border Collies won't cause any problems if they're taken outside.

Keepers need to provide adequate exercise opportunity for a working dog like the Border Collie. You need to take them out for a walk at least twice a day. If you don't have that time to take them out every day, make sure that you have a backyard where they can roam around and explore their thirst for adventure.

Chapter One: All About the Collies

They are people - pleaser

Collies are generally people – pleasers. You can expect them to always do their best to make you and your family happy; all they ask of course is that you give them your attention, time, and love!

Young Collie breeds sometimes go through sort of a juvenile period where they challenge their keepers for dominance and they show stubbornness which is why you need to have a firm training at this age so that you can help your Border Collie pup be disciplined.

Since Border Collies are naturally inclined to do work, and they are quite independent animals, they will usually find ways to do something if you are not playing with them or if you don't give them something to divert their energy on. They might end up digging your garden and backyard, or they could also end up chewing house furniture which is why providing them with exercising opportunities or playing a game of fetch at least twice or thrice a week will surely make them feel as if they are pleasing you, and it also avoid behavioral problems.

Chapter One: All About the Collies

Dealing with Children and Other Household Pets

As mentioned earlier, it's best that you take time to properly socialize your pet so that they can get along well with other potential pets and people in general. Border collies are more suited for older kids than young ones because collies can easily get startled as they are quite sensitive to screams and loud noises. And since Border Collies have a tendency to keep things in order, your pet may tend to nip or growl at your child if he/she cannot be controlled.

In general though, if your children learn to work with your pet, they can surely have a great time playing with one another and this can be a great exercising opportunity both for your dog and your kid. You'll find that collies are quite protective once they form a bond with you or your family. They tend to bark against people they don't know or if a stranger is approaching you.

Border Collies gets along with other household pets like cats or dogs provided of course that they are properly introduced and socialized. Since Border Collies are a large – sized breed, they will tend to have a better relationship with larger breed dogs compared to smaller toy breeds as they could have dominant tendencies.

It's best to keep two Border Collies, preferably a male and female, that's both neutered and around 1 year apart. If they are not neutered/ spayed then they will most likely have territoriality issues or even unwanted pregnancies! Make sure to supervise your pet dog with another pet, be it a dog or cat, until you are sure that they're safe to be left with one another or until their relationship is already established. Keep in mind that Border Collies are natural herders which could be a source of conflict with other animals.

Competitions

If you want your collie to enter dog competitions such as herding competitions, athletic events, fly – dog, and obedience competitions, you can expect them to excel at these kinds of events provided of course that you help them when it comes to training and other athletic/ intelligence demands that these competitions require.

Chapter One: All About the Collies

Border collies could get intimidated by large crowds and other animals around which is why it's best to socialize them so that they are comfortable when joining events. If you are considering your pet to compete, it's probably best to hire a professional dog trainer so that your dog can maximize its potential. Competitions will be a rewarding experience for both you and y our dog, such events can also form a strong and bonded relationship. Good luck!

Chapter Two: Choosing a Border Collie

Now that you've learn the origin and biological information of the Border Collies, it's time to learn how to choose the right Border Collie dog for you. This chapter will tackle the pros and cons of getting either a male or female collie. You need to factor in the characteristics that male and female dogs will have so that you can make an informed choice. Picking the cutest – looking pup is the most common mistake that newbie keepers do so try to avoid that. This chapter will help you determine which gender is best suited for you, and you'll also learn the benefits and difficulties of purchasing the Border Collie as a puppy versus as an adult dog. Considering your options beforehand along with the factors involved such as your environment, budget, time etc. will enable you to make the best choice.

Male or Female?

Pros and Cons of Owning a Male Collie

- Males are generally larger which means that they would eat more – which also means that you need to buy more food compared to female collies.

- Males are much stronger, bulkier, and taller than females. This could be a concern if you have smaller – size pets around like poodles or small cat breeds.

- Male collies will eat more food compared to non – pregnant female collies.

- Males are usually more aggressive and also independent.

Chapter Two: Choosing a Border Collie

- Male collies may be quite difficult to manage if you only live in a small and confined house because they won't have outlet for their energy.

- Males generally have territoriality issues especially if there's another male species around. This is also true if there are female dogs around that are in their heat period.

- Males usually establish a close relationship to their owner compared to females that can equally form a bond with people other than their main keeper.

- Males will require more exercise and playtime. They also tend to be more difficult to introduce to new pets and socialize compared to female collies.

- Male collies reach sexual maturity earlier than females. Their sexual tendencies can already be seen at a young age, and this could be a problem if you own other female dog breeds.

- Don't be surprise if your male collie roams around the house or even in your neighborhood because this means that they probably have smelled a female dog that's in heat and they're pursuing it.

Breeding Concerns of Male Collies

Neutering your male collie will eliminate any concerns regarding unwanted pregnancies. However, if you are interested in breeding your dog, you have to make sure that you secure him in a solid fence even if he's still small. If you buy a pair of dogs (male and female) for breeding, you have to make sure that you monitor the male dog because they often show aggression when a female dog is in heat.

Males are naturally possessive to their female counterparts even towards its keepers. This could be a concern if you have young kids around the house, or if you don't have your dogs in an enclosure. If ever your female dog doesn't respond to your male dog's advances, your male collie may also become aggressive.

Chapter Two: Choosing a Border Collie
Pros and Cons of Owning a Female Collie

- Female dogs are smaller in size and are generally less aggressive. Most female dogs only become aggressive when they gave birth to their pups but this is because they're just protecting their litter.

- Female dogs are less active compared to male collies and they are also generally easier to train.

- They usually gets shy and scared if anyone treated them in a harsh way or scold them in an angry voice.

- They tend to get along with people other than their owners.

- They are easier to introduce and socialize with other household pets.

- They usually don't get along if they are housed with another female, and this may result to conflict which is why it's best to pair them up with a male if you want to keep two Border Collies.

- Group of female Border Collies will form a hierarchy, and will bond with each other once the pecking order is established.

Breeding Concerns of Female Collies

Females will come into their heat period twice a year. It usually lasts for about 3 weeks. Expect to see a fluid discharge from them as this is designed to attract a male Collie. If you have your female spayed, this will prevent male dogs in smelling the heat.

Similarities

Generally speaking, both male and female Border Collies should be given equal amount of effort, time, and attention especially in socializing and training. They will require the same amount of exercise, feeding, play time, general care, housing, and love. You will need to make sure that they receive yearly vaccinations and routine checkups from the vet.

Chapter Two: Choosing a Border Collie

Choosing whether you want a male or female dog is entirely up to your preference. Use the pros and cons aforementioned before you make a decision. It's also important to note that if you don't plan on breeding your pet Collies, it's best for them to be spayed or neutered so that they won't be pursued by other dog breeds and prevent any sexual tendencies, and unwanted pregnancies.

Puppy or Adult?

The next thing you need to decide on prior to buying a Border Collie is to know whether you should get a pup or a more matured dog. This section will provide you with the pros and cons of purchasing a puppy versus an adult Border Collie. Taking the time to consider the pros and cons is very important at the onset in order to avoid any problems in the future particularly in terms of general care and budget. For instance, you may need to consider asking yourself the following questions if you plan on buying a pup instead of an adult:

- Do you think you can have the time to train a puppy?
- How much time can you set aside for puppy training?

Chapter Two: Choosing a Border Collie

- Are you patient when it comes to working with young canines?
- Do you have the budget to meet the needs of the pup?
- Do you have time to play and interact with them on a daily basis?

These are just some of the questions you may need to ponder on. Now, let's go to the pros and cons of owning a pup, and an adult on the next section.

Pros and Cons of Owning a Collie Puppy

- Puppies are obviously the cutest and most adorable stage in any dog's life. If you want to soak in their lovable and energetic personalities then consider getting a pup instead of an adult. Young collies will surely brighten you and your family's day the moment you wake up in the morning.

- Getting a puppy is best suited for individuals and families who can spend quality time with a young dog. If you plan on raising your Border Collie according to your standards, and you're focus on

Chapter Two: Choosing a Border Collie

properly training them to meet you/ your family's want or needs, then you'll have better chances with a pup compared to an adult.

- You need to spend quality time with your Collie pup and form a bond with them so that they will be easier to train or socialize. Some people get a pup but they are not in the house all the time or they don't take the time to train them, and they wonder why their pets are misbehaving. If you want your Collie to become a well – behaved pet as it grows, you must give time and attention to it, and not just provide their basic needs.

- Buying a puppy from a reputable source or rescue shelter will make the dog stay longer as part of your family since it'll recognize that you're the one providing them with all their basic needs and general care as they grow. They'll recognize that they're part of the pack.

Chapter Two: Choosing a Border Collie

- Prior to buying a puppy from the breeder, it's best that you take the time to see how they interact and play with other dogs as this will give you a hint when it comes to temperament/ personality. Usually, puppies who grew in a litter tend to be more assertive and aggressive than puppies who are raised alone which is why the former might be harder to train. The latter though may tend to be more reserved especially with strangers, which is why socialization at an early age is important.

- Some owners find it difficult to manage and raise a pup especially if they have their own families to take care of. You have to keep in mind that raising a puppy whether it's a Collie breed or not is very similar to having a baby. You are responsible 24/7 especially in the first few months.

- You need to ensure that you have the time to let your pup meet new people, other pets, and take them out for a walk around the neighborhood. As puppies grow, you'll soon find out that they also go through

Chapter Two: Choosing a Border Collie

the "stubborn stage" just like a child. If you're sort of a neat freak and you want everything organize around the house, getting a puppy may not be best for you because at some point they can damage your furniture and other household items especially when they undergo the "chewing stage." You need to puppy – proof your house and also housebreak your pup.

- If you want training to be effective, you have to be consistent with your methods and the schedule otherwise it could be difficult for you and your pup. You have to have lots of patience if you plan on getting a pup.

Pros and Cons of Owning an Adult

- Some keepers find it more advantageous to acquire an adult Border Collie because you easily know its overall appearance and size as well as its personality and behavior. Most adult dogs are socialized, trained and housebroken already which means that it can

Chapter Two: Choosing a Border Collie

save you time and skip all the difficult parts of dog keeping – not to mention your patience and furniture!

- If you acquire your adult Collie from a reputable breeder, the dog will most likely be trained already. You can expect him/her to already know how to behave around the house, on the leash, or whenever you're out for a walk. Training is still a must but it'll be less time consuming since they're already matured compared to training a pup. Same amount of love and care is needed but less emphasis on training concepts.

- Most matured Collies tend to be calmer when introduced to a new surrounding which is why you won't have a problem once you bring your pet home although introduction, socialization, and housebreaking must still be taught. An adult collie may take just a few days to adjust to its new environment so just give them time to settle and bond with them often so that they will get to establish a relationship with you and your family.

Chapter Two: Choosing a Border Collie

- The biggest disadvantage of buying an adult dog is that it'll be harder to change any of the negative behavior they may have. If you find that your dog adapted a bad habit from its previous owner, it might be very difficult to correct. It's still possible to re – train your dog but it could be confusing for your pet. You will need to take effort if you want to change a particular habit you don't like and encourage them with treats or use positive reinforcement. Patience is a must if this is going to be your problem.

- If you find that your adult Collie doesn't listen to you or are showing signs of misbehaving, make sure to take the time to give them positive attention and socialize with them so that they'll develop a good relationship with you. Some adults may find it hard to settle in a new environment and this is where they usually become difficult to handle.

- Adult Collies may also be harder to introduce and/ or socialize with your other household pets, which is why you need to ensure that you monitor them

Chapter Two: Choosing a Border Collie

whenever they're interacting with one another. If you have a smaller breed of dogs or cats, it might be more difficult since Border Collies tend to herd things and show dominance to smaller animals.

- When it comes to basic needs, it's almost the same with puppies. Make sure that your adult dog is getting the right amount of food, has enough space around the house where they can have exercising opportunities, and that their health is taken care of. You will need to make sure that they're neutered/spayed to avoid any aggressive behavior or unwanted pregnancies.

Chapter Three: Acquiring a Border Collie

A dog breeder isn't like a veterinarian, teacher or a lawyer; you can't measure a breeder by checking if they have any training recognition or any sort of educational attainment related to breeding animals because the standard of being a reputable breeder is based on the temperament and overall health of the pups they raised. Most animal breeders do this job not for the purpose of just making a quick buck but because they truly are passionate about breeding a particular canine. They have a genuine love and compassion for the dogs they breed, and always act in the best interest of the individual pups they raise.

Chapter Three: Acquiring a Border Collie

If you want to acquire the best Border Collie breed, you have to ensure that you only buy it from a reputable and responsible breeder. This chapter will guide you on how to identify one, and also give you other options should you choose to buy from other sources. You'll also learn the purchase price of Border Collies as well as how you can legally acquire them.

The Reputable Breeder Detector

There are two kinds of animal breeders; one is only concern about the money that they'll get from it while the other is more concern on how to advance the breed – and they treat their pups as if it's one of their own, they want to make sure that their babies are going to good and responsible keepers. You can easily detect which are the reputable breeders by simply asking them a couple of questions. In fact, you can already know if they are reputable or a responsible breeder if they themselves ask you a question.

Chapter Three: Acquiring a Border Collie

Make sure to ask the following questions to your prospective breeder:

- **Do you have a contract?** (The contract must clearly outline a refund policy and health guarantees – more on this later).

- **Do you know the history of the pups' parents?** (The breeder should know who the parents are so that you can ask for a lineage chart to know if the puppy is from a healthy family).

- **Can you show me the breeding or kennel area?** (You have to check if the kennel is sanitary, animal friendly and more than adequate for the litters).

- **Are you recognized by any local/ national breeding organization or dog club for the Border Collie breed?** (It's better if the breeder is a member of any dog club or is recognized by a breeding organization

Chapter Three: Acquiring a Border Collie

because this is an indication that they adhere to the breed's standards).

- **How often do you breed your male/ female Collies? How many times do they reproduce in a year?** (Dogs should be bred at least once a year only, and the current limit of per bitch is only six).

These are some of the questions you need to ask your prospective breeder. Keep in mind that the breeder you choose should be first and foremost concerned with the health and safety of their litter. They will only allow serious buyers to handle their pups. Expect them to also ask you some questions regarding your job, time etc. because this is how they will know if you too are a responsible keeper.

Other Sources and Purchase Price

Pet Stores

Various pet stores sell Border Collie breed and it ranges around $200 to $400 which is around the same price

Chapter Three: Acquiring a Border Collie

that legit breeders are offering for their pups. However, we don't recommend acquiring your Border Collie from pet stores because there's usually very little information on where they came from. You won't be sure of its health, and the dog's temperament. In addition to that, pups that are being sold to pet stores usually come from puppy mills that are mass breeding dogs, and are not being taken care of health wise.

Rescues

There are various rescue centers in the U.S. and even in the U.K that houses abandoned Border Collie dogs. Rescue centers are built to help find new home for abandoned dog breeds. Depending on where you live, you may find a Border Collie that you prefer. They usually house young and adult breeds as well as senior dogs.

Perhaps the main advantage of acquiring your pet from rescue centers is that you already have an idea of the kind of temperament/ behavior the dog has. On top of that they are usually well taken care of; dogs from rescue shelters

Chapter Three: Acquiring a Border Collie

are already vaccinated and sometimes neutered/ spayed already.

Some rescue center will charge you with a basic fee for you to legally adopt the abandoned Border Collie. It will cost you just about $100 to $200. The price will depend on the shelter and/ or the length of time that dog stayed with them. Sometimes they will also ask an additional donation if ever the dog required a special treatment from the vet. Usually, dogs from rescue centers are in poor health but because they are well – taken care of, you can be quite sure that they are already healthy and well – trained once they are adopted out. Vets usually volunteer to take care of the dogs in rescue centers. The money you'll donate is used to provide the needed food and meds for future rescue animals.

Legit Breeders

The best option is to really acquire your Border Collie from a breeder that's an expert in this particularly canine. You can find lots of Border Collie breeder across the country. Although it may cost a bit more expensive compared to

Chapter Three: Acquiring a Border Collie

buying from pet stores or adopting from rescue shelters, you can be sure of the dog's quality. The cost of the puppy will depend on the following factors:

- Trial performance of the pups' parents.
- Lineage of both parents
- Reputation of the breeder itself (the more in - demand they are, the pricier they could get).
- The color of the coat and also the markings of the pup (the more unique, the more expensive it will be)
- Championship lines of Border Collies are usually more expensive than non – performance dog breeds.

Non – performance Border Collie puppies may cost anywhere between $225 and $600 while puppies from Championship lineages may cost anywhere between $800 and $1,000.

Keep in mind that there could be additional expense for shipping costs. Most legit breeders already have their pups micro - chipped prior to purchasing. The health certificates

Chapter Three: Acquiring a Border Collie

and registration papers/ contract are already included in the price of a purebred Collie pup.

Contracts

As mentioned earlier, it's very importantn that you ask your breeder to come up with a contract because it will serve as the bill of sale for your Border Collie pup. The contract must clearly state the rights that have been agreed upon by you and your breeder. The contract is a binding agreement so make sure that before you sign, you have already asked any concerns you might have before you finalize everything. Here are some of the things included in the contract:

A Bill of Sale

This bill of sale is very important because this will be your proof of dog ownership. Make sure that you understand the legal aspects before purchasing a puppy or dog. Many places in the U.S. require animals to have a health report to ensure that the puppy is getting the right health vaccinations.

Chapter Three: Acquiring a Border Collie

If you find that your pet is unhealthy, you can still return it to the breeder within 48 hours. This will depend on your binding agreement with the breeder and what the law will require in your area of residence.

Registration Application

This part of the contract is filled out by the breeder/seller. He/ she needs to fill in the details of the breed (ex: sex, color, physical characteristics, date of birth, name of parents, registration numbers, other health – related info). The breeder will need to include their name or their business' name, and it must be affix with the seller's signature.

Health Guarantee

This part of the contract should state that the breeder has ensured that the dog is free from any diseases (both genetic and hereditary conditions) that may not be present at the time of your purchase.

Lineage Chart

The seller must provide a lineage statement or attached a copy of the pup's lineage chart. This is very important if you bought a Championship Border Collie breed.

Additional Clauses in the Contract

Here are other clauses/ information that could be stated in the contract:

Breeding Restrictions

It should be best that the seller/ breeder state if the puppy you're getting is either spayed or neutered. The seller might also state that the dog must not be bred until it reaches 2 years old, and if you plan in doing so, the breeder should be consulted first. This is usually done to make sure that other people will not breed dogs inappropriately, and so that the blood line remains strong.

Showing Dogs

The seller may indicate in the contract that the dog must be shown at least a few times per year. On the other hand, you would want to make sure that the contract

Chapter Three: Acquiring a Border Collie

guarantees that your pet can reproduce and the offspring will be free from hereditary concerns.

Health Notification

Many breeders that are concerned with improving the lines of their breed may require that you notify them if ever there are any health issues that will come up after buying the dog. They may also require for an autopsy if ever the dog suddenly dies due to unforeseen death.

Selling or Giving the Pup/ Dog

Most reputable breeders will also include in the contract that should you choose to stop caring for the dog for some reason, the pup/ dog will be returned to them. This could mean that you cannot sell or give the pet away without first asking them. This is usually a good sign because that means the breeder you're buying from is really committed in keeping their animals safe and happy.

Carefully reading the contract you've agreed to will surely make you feel confident about the Border Collie breed you're purchasing. Perhaps one of the best ways to really

Chapter Three: Acquiring a Border Collie

detect a good breeder is when he/she take the time to discuss the written agreement with you and address any concerns you may have.

Chapter Four: Bringing Home Your New Border Collie

You've already learned a thing or two about where and how you can acquire your very own Border Collie, now it's time to bring him home. Bringing home your newfound pet as sweet and charming as a Collie will surely be an exciting time for you and your family. This chapter will cover some tips on how you can help your new pup or matured dog make the transition to its new home. You'll learn the basic supplies they will need and guidelines on how to puppy/ dog – proof your house to keep them safe from any potential harm inside the household.

Chapter Four: Bringing Home Your New Border Collie

Bringing home a puppy is going to be a different experience compared to bringing an adult Border Collie home. Learn about what to expect once they've finally set their paws into their new home.

Bringing Home a Border Collie Pup

It's always very exciting once a new member of the family arrives especially when it's as cute and cuddly as a young puppy! However, first time dog owners aren't usually aware of how challenging the first few days can be especially when bringing home a young pup.

If you want to avoid getting frustrated and exhausted once your new pup arrives, it's better to plan ahead of time and prepare your house for him/ her. You will need to puppy – proof your home in order to provide a hazard - free environment for your young pup. You'll need just a few hours to make your house safe once your pet arrives; puppy – proofing will set the tone for you and your pup's relationship, and will create a proper introduction to the family as well.

Chapter Four: Bringing Home Your New Border Collie

In addition to puppy – proofing your house, you need to also prepare the basic supplies that your puppy will need at least a few days before its scheduled arrival. You'll also need to prepare yourself because working with puppies can be quite exhausting as well. Having the right attitude and a plan especially when it comes to feeding/ exercise/ grooming/ training schedules etc. will help you get things in order and save you time. The key is to enjoy the caring process, be extra patient, and just love them for who they are.

Basic Puppy Supplies

Before bringing your puppy home, it's important that basic supplies are already prepared because this will make your puppy feel safe. Make sure to ask the breeder/ previous owner as to what kind of diet the puppy was raised in, if the pup has any special requirements, habits etc. Basic supplies include the following:

- A guide book on how to care for Border Collie pups (by reading this book, you already have this covered!)

Chapter Four: Bringing Home Your New Border Collie

- Ask your breeder if the puppy already began training, if so, then make sure to continue the training to avoid confusion with the already established commands.

- Dog crate. It must be at least twice as large as the current size of your pup.

- Bedding Material. It's best that you buy quality bedding that can't be easily destroyed. Make sure it's washable because it'll be prone to your pup's litter.

- Puppy Collar. A woven or materials made out of soft fabric is preferred. Make sure that the collar you buy has a buckle fastener so that you can fit your puppy's neck without it being too loose or tight. A good measurement is if you can easily insert your 2 fingers between the collar and your pup's neck.

- Quality lead. This is a must especially when you take your pup out for a walk. It's highly recommended

Chapter Four: Bringing Home Your New Border Collie

that you buy a retractable type of lead to make the dog easier to handle.

- ID Tag. This will serve as an identification if ever your puppy gets lost. Make sure to put it on their collar and include your contact details so that your puppy can be easily returned to you. This is a must even if your dog is already micro – chipped.

- Grooming Supplies. The things you'll need for grooming will depend if your pet's coat is longhaired or shorthaired. Make sure to ask the breeder regarding what age can you start trimming your pup's coat. Usually, you need to wait until the puppy is already 10 months old. Ask your vet or breeder about it.

- Puppy Toys. This is a must both for pups and even dogs. Toys will keep dog boredom at bay and it'll keep them occupied if you aren't available to play with them. The toys should preferably be plastic and

Chapter Four: Bringing Home Your New Border Collie

doesn't become a choking hazard. If your puppy is happy with his/ her toys, he/ she will refrain from chewing household items or furniture.

- Good quality of puppy food. Make sure to have this ready once your pup arrives. You need to ask your breeder as to what kind of diet your pup has and try to continue that by buying the same brand or offering the same amount. If you want to change their diet, make sure to do it in a gradual way so as not to upset your pup's stomach. What you can do is to combine the old diet with the new so that transition is gradual. Let your pup adjust to the new diet to prevent diarrhea.

- Plastic/ Stainless Food and Water Bowl. Since pups are quite active animals, you need to make sure that you buy a food/ water bowl that can't be easily tipped over. Make sure to replenish clean water 2 times a day. Some keepers use automatic feeders but it's just optional.

Chapter Four: Bringing Home Your New Border Collie

- Baby Gates. If you want to confine your pup in one area then purchasing baby gates is very ideal. This will prevent your curious pup in accessing restricted areas around the house.

- Spray – on No - Chew products. This will come in handy if your pet is fond of chewing one of your furniture or any potentially hazardous material.

Safety Tips

Having a puppy is just like having a baby in the house which is why you need to make sure that your house is safe because they are naturally curious at this stage and will definitely go through everything. Simple cords or hanging curtains can be a hazard for your pet; here are some safety tips for your new pup:

- Pick up cords or any kind of strings lying around the house. These materials can easily be swallowed by your pet and can definitely cause stomach problems.

Chapter Four: Bringing Home Your New Border Collie

- Remove any choking hazard. Small pieces of toys and something similar must be removed because your pup will be curious enough to swallow them.

- Check the houseplants. If you have cactus inside the house, make sure it's out of reach. Check if the plants are poisonous for your pet, and if so, better place them elsewhere or completely remove them.

- Keep electrical cords or any potentially hazardous material out of reach. Simple materials like matches, lighters, fire extinguishers etc. must be secured. Don't let your pup access them if you want to make sure that you still have a house to go home to. Spraying a no – chew product to the cords or other materials will make it unpleasant for the pup.

- Keep the puppy lock up inside its kennel if you're going to be out for a while or if you're unable to watch the puppy. Make sure to provide food, water and toys.

Chapter Four: Bringing Home Your New Border Collie

Bringing Home an Adult Border Collie

Bringing home a full – grown or matured dog doesn't need quite as much attention compared to bringing home a pup. Adult Border Collies are usually house - broken already and some are also trained and well – behave. However, you still need to take precautions and let your pet adjust to its new environment. Provide him/ her with the following supplies:

Basic Border Collie Supplies

- Stainless/ plastic food and water dishes.

- Kennel/ Crate. Most keepers prefer that their dog stays in his/ her kennel and not just let the dog sleep anywhere in the house but this of course is up to you. However, providing a kennel will make your Border Collie feel safe and comfortable.

- Washable bedding material

Chapter Four: Bringing Home Your New Border Collie

- Collar, ID Tag, and lead. For larger Border Collie dogs, you can use a chain collar but make sure to be careful with it as it could hurt your pet if you pull them off while walking. This is why retractable leashes are preferred because your dog will have freedom to roam around while you're still maintaining control over him/ her.

- Quality Dog Food. (We will discuss more about this on the next chapter).

- Dog Toys.

Crate Training Your Border Collie

- Learn to praise your dog. Keep in mind that your voice is first and foremost your training tool. You need to also consider using a consistent phrase to cue your pet to go inside its crate. Pairing a word/ phrase will help when you're instructing your pet and catching their attention towards where it needs to be.

Chapter Four: Bringing Home Your New Border Collie

- You should initially use a lock or something so that the door wouldn't swing back and forth so that it wouldn't scare your Border Collie.

- Lure them with toys and treats! Keeping a bowl of treats when you're doing crate training will be handy because it will function as pre – bait for your dog. Chew toys is also essential because you'll need to reward it afterwards. Never crate train your dog if you don't have food and toy rewards. You must set it up beforehand so that it can be convenient for you once you start training your Collie.

- Avoid following a strict routine when crate training your Collie. Routines are great but make sure that your training follow – up is not predictable for your pet. What you need to do is to destabilize any pattern that will short – circuit your dog's expectation. This way it will help preserve the integrity of your crate training.

Chapter Four: Bringing Home Your New Border Collie

- Crate training is quite a labor intensive task but it lessens the onset of many problems in the long run. Observe your dog as it will have its own pace of learning. You need to be patient and continue practicing your pet to go to the crate willingly. It may probably take several days to a few weeks or maybe even longer so don't rush it.

Dog – Proofing Your Home

- If you are keeping other household pets, it's best to separate your Border Collie once it arrives to avoid any fights. Once you've properly socialize your dog with your family, you can start introducing him to your other pets but do so with precaution and make sure that you monitor their interaction.

- It's also best for you to dog – proof your house at least until you already have an idea on how your Border Collie behaves around the house. Remove any chewable items or any appliances that they can get

Chapter Four: Bringing Home Your New Border Collie

caught up in. Secure electrical cords and anything that's hanging as well as the food in your kitchen. Once your Border Collie dog already demonstrated a well – behave manner, you may place the items back in the room.

- If you have children around the house make sure to supervise them when interacting with an adult Border Collie. The dog may be quite wary to children and will need to adjust before your kids can freely pet or play with them. Adult Border Collies are not advisable for very young kids as these dogs tend to herd things including humans. Make sure to not stimulate or over excite your Border Collie at least for the first few days so that they can properly adjust.

Chapter Four: Bringing Home Your New Border Collie

Chapter Five: Border Collie's Basic Needs

This chapter will focus on two of the most important basic needs of your pet; exercise and diet. The things you'll learn in the following sections are essential to keeping your dog's health at its optimum. You'll need to consider your pet's current condition, age, and preferences before changing their diet or setting up an exercise routine for them. We also highly recommend that before you change anything, you should first consult the vet or the breeder so that you'll have an idea if you're doing the right thing. Proper exercise and diet is very important for your pet's overall wellness & longevity.

Chapter Five: Border Collie's Basic Needs

Exercise Needs

Exercise is not just important for us humans, it's also one of your Collie's basic needs. Providing them with exercise opportunities contributes to a healthy well – being. All dogs need exercise though some will require more amount than others. If you want to prevent your Border Collie from becoming obese and acquiring illnesses in the long term, then make sure to start your Collie on a regular exercise routine. Here are some of the benefits of getting your Collie to exercise:

- Sine Border Collies are energetic pets, exercise is a great and proper outlet for them.
- They'll be more content with their life.
- Collies will become more alert
- They would sleep better
- Exercise will contribute to a longer life span
- Exercise will help build strong muscles and bones and it will also improve their cardiovascular system.

Chapter Five: Border Collie's Basic Needs

If you acquired a Collie pup, it's best to start them with scheduled walks and play time. Just allow your dog to run around your backyard or in a confined area. On the other hand, if you bought an adult Border Collie, you may need to encourage them when it comes to exercising because they won't run around as much as a Collie pup.

Your Border Collie may also get their exercise by simply playing with your other household pets. You may sugar coat exercise with play time so that your dog will not dread the process. Aside from going out for walks, take the time to play fetch with them or better yet create an obstacle playground then give them treats and praises whenever they finish the challenge for the day.

Factors to Consider When Exercising Your Collie

The level and kind of exercise for your pet Collie will depend on their age, physical condition, and health needs. Make sure to ask your vet as to how much exercise your dog needs every day. Consider the following factors:

Chapter Five: Border Collie's Basic Needs

Your Dog's Age

Young pups and senior Border Collies will require their own exercise routines in order to avoid strain and mishaps. What you can do to ensure that your pet doesn't get restrained or do excessive amounts of exercise especially when walking them is to make sure that you include lots of stops around the park or in the street; this goes for both very young pups and older Collie dogs. Make sure to supervise them when playing with another pet to avoid rough play or excessive running. Keep your senior Collie away from a more active pet to avoid exhaustion.

Your Dog's Physical Condition

Border Collies are known to be hard workers but sometimes they are as lazy as a "couch potato." This is the reason why you need to start off your dog in a gradual way when it comes to exercising so that it won't be too much for them. Here are some things you can do:

- Take your dog out for at least a 15 minute walk at least twice a day.

Chapter Five: Border Collie's Basic Needs

- Monitor your dog's condition during the exercise. Watch for any signs of wheezing, distress, panting etc. because some breeds including Border Collies have trouble breathing whenever they are exerting effort on themselves, so if you see your dog starts to catch its breath, it's probably best to take a rest or make the walks shorter or include lots of stops. The important thing is to make it short but frequent so that your dog will get enough exercise without tiring themselves.

- Keep in mind that it could be hard to exercise a short – legged dog together with a long - legged dog because they obviously require different amounts of exercise. One of your pet could be more exhausted than the other so make sure to factor that in when planning your exercise routines.

- Never walk your dog right after eating because this might cause them to regurgitate their food or experience digestive problems.

Chapter Five: Border Collie's Basic Needs

- It's ideal to brisk walk your pet for at least around 30 minutes twice a day. If you're in shape and your Border Collie doesn't have any health problems, you can try a slow jog with them. This is a great way to keep you and your pet healthy while spending bonding time together.

- Go to the vet if you find that your dog have difficulty exercising. Your pet may require a change in their diet or undergo through a weight loss program.

- Check your pet's paws or foot pads as he/ she can accumulate gravel, stones, or ice over time. This could be painful and definitely a hindrance during walks or exercise.

Provide Variety

It's very important to stick to an exercise routine but many keepers recommend that you also add a bit of variety from time to time so as not to make it predictable for your dog. Check out some activities below that you can add to 'spice up' your dog's exercise routine:

Chapter Five: Border Collie's Basic Needs

- Do some Frisbee chasing

- Walk your dog to a new park or an unfamiliar area around the neighborhood

- Jog for a few minutes then go back to brisk walking

- Take your Border Collie to an obedience class so that he/she can learn new tricks and other training methods.

Dangerous Activities

There are times when you see other dog owners exercising their dogs in ways that are potentially dangerous to both the keeper and their pet. Follow some of the don'ts whenever you're exercising or playing with your dog:

- Never exercise your dog while you're cycling, skateboarding, driving, roller skating or doing similar dangerous activities because there had been instances that caused accidents and injuries concerning the dog's leash becoming tangled.

- Never exercise your pet during very humid days or in the middle of the day because it will cause your Collie to become dehydrated. If you're going out for a walk during hot days, make sure to bring water for your pet or plan a route where your Collie can have the opportunity to quench its thirst. Some dog breeds can experience heatstroke due to humid temperatures, dehydration and/ or exhaustion from exercise. Watch out for signs of heatstroke, this includes rapid and heavy breathing, excessive salivation, and staggering gait.

Dietary Needs

When giving nutrition for your Border Collie, just make sure that you never feed your pet more than the amount he/ she needs. Consult your breeder and you're your veterinarian for advice on whether your Border Collie needs more food or maybe additional supplements and vitamins. Don't make the mistake of feeding your Border Collie more or less food just because of his/ her appearance.

Chapter Five: Border Collie's Basic Needs

Carnivores or Omnivores?

Some keepers think that dog breeds are omnivores because they eat both veggies and meat which is a fact but that's only because they would pretty much eat anything. Keep in mind that canines are carnivores by nature. Their digestive system is naturally set to digest meat since they have strong and powerful digestive juices.

Dogs in general are designed to eat flesh meat. If you study their anatomy, dogs have short intestines and they also have strong jaw bones, and sharp teeth that are meant to cut and rip meats. Although they can eat other type of foods like vegetables or human scrapes, their primary diet should be carnivorous.

The Diet Switch

Most keepers switch foods once their puppies hit 9 months. We highly recommend that you first consult your breeder or vet before changing your Border Collie's diet so that you can be sure as to what age is appropriate for the diet switch. Some people introduce adult food earlier than nine months, while some do it a little over ten months which is why it's best to ask your vet or breeder since they already have knowledge and experience regarding this matter.

Wet vs. Dry Food

One of the first things that you need to consider when it comes to feeding your Border Collie is whether you should feed dry or wet food, or perhaps a combination of both.

Well, there are actually pros and cons to feeding both types of these foods. Wet food is often preferred by dogs of all ages. Most keepers feed their Border Collie pups and senior dogs with wet food because it's much easier to digest than dry food.

Vets also recommend feeding wet food for at least a few days whenever your Border Collie is experiencing digestive or dental problems. However, vets as well as breeders do not recommend that wet food should be the only diet of your pet because wet food will not contain the same consistency and fiber that dry food offers. If you feed your Border Collie with only wet food, your dog might

Chapter Five: Border Collie's Basic Needs

defecate often and produce excessive gas which is why you need to balance it with dry food diet.

If your pup starts off with a wet food and you want to switch them over to eating dry food, you can do so by mixing the wet food with dry food so that your dog can gradually adjust to eating this diet. Feeding your Border Collie with dry food will promote a healthy digestion and cleaner teeth.

Whenever you feed your dog with dry food, make sure that you provide him/her access to fresh water. The dry food should not contain any wheat or corn because it can swell up your Collie's tummy.

It's best to ask your vet on what kind of premium brands you should feed your dog. Make sure that the brand you're going to buy will contain balanced nutrients and will have appropriate amounts of proteins, carbs, fatty acids, vitamins, and minerals.

Scheduled Feeding Vs. Free Feeding

Once you have decided on what kind of food you're going to feed your Border Collie, the next step is to decide

Chapter Five: Border Collie's Basic Needs

how you're going to feed them. Most keepers schedule their dog's feeding. Scheduled feeding is when the food of your Collie is offered for up to 20 minutes only before removing it whether it's eaten by your pet or not. This is quite an effective habit especially for indoor pets because it also helps you out when planning for their walks, play time, and exercise breaks.

On the other hand, free feeding is when you simply place an automatic feeder or offer your pet with a bowl of food that they can access whenever they want. Free feeding is usually the culprit to obesity because your pet can eat anytime he/ she wants. Free feeding may not be a good idea if you have other pets/ dogs inside the house because they could steal food from one another. The dominant dog usually has the 'authority' to eat the food of the submissive dogs. This could start conflicts and aggression towards your pets. If you choose free feeding, make sure that their food bowls are placed in their own crates and the other pets won't have any access to it other than their own feeders.

Chapter Five: Border Collie's Basic Needs

Home Cooking for Your Border Collie

You can also try to cook for your Border Collie every now and then to provide a varied diet. Here are some ingredients that you can include in your Border Collie's home – cooked diet:

- Carrots
- Broccoli
- Minced Turkey
- Apples
- Minced Chicken
- Raw chicken with bones
- Beef chunks
- Egg

Home – Cooking Steps

Step #1: Mix the first the couple of veggies like the carrots, apples, and broccoli.

Step #2: Chop the veggies to about a few pieces, mix it with a bit of water, and blend it. Then you can place the minced turkey or chicken on the food bowl as ease, and pour in the blended veggie juices.

Chapter Five: Border Collie's Basic Needs

Step #3: Slightly mash and mix the veggies juices with the meat.

Step #4: Add the egg because it's also a great source of protein for your pet.

Step #5: Add chicken with bone on top of that. Keep in mind that the amount you give should depend on your pet's current size.

Step #6: Add in dog multivitamins once or twice a day depending on what your vet tells you.

Additional Tips:

- You can also buy a ready – made mixed fruit and vegetable and add it on your minced chicken or turkey, chicken bone, and egg so that you won't have to chop up individual veggies or fruits.

- You can also opt to use the egg shells because it's also a great source of calcium.

Chapter Five: Border Collie's Basic Needs

Grooming Needs

Bathing Guidelines

Canines don't like bathing in general especially if you're living an area where there are really cold temperatures. Some keepers bathe their dogs every other week or more often, it's entirely up to you and the living condition you have but just don't do it on a frequent basis Here are some guidelines on how you can properly bathe your Border Collie:

- Brush off all the loose fur/coat, and make sure that there are no mats. Brush their coat a bit before soaking it with water. Blow drying can also blow away the residue and loose fur in your pet's coat. Use a coat rake to brush him and entangle carefully any loose furs. The goal of brushing though is to always get rid of the loose hair and keep the coat smooth and clean.

Chapter Five: Border Collie's Basic Needs

- Prepare your dog toiletries such as towel, rubber mat, shampoo, soap, water etc., after you've brushed your Collie's coat.

- Make sure that you provide a rubber mat or a towel to prevent him from slipping off. If you're going to bathe your Collie outside, it's really not necessary to put a rubber mat but it can still be useful.

- Wet your dog with lukewarm water. It'll probably take around ten minutes to wet him all over. Once you've done that, you can now apply the dog soap or dog shampoo. However, before you do make sure that it's diluted with water.

- After you rub and bathe your Border Collie, it's time to rinse him off. Make sure that there's no trace of shampoo left as it could irritate your pet and make him/ her itch.

- Dry him off using a towel and blow dryer. Dry him off and use a blow dryer to dry the water on his skin.

Chapter Five: Border Collie's Basic Needs

Additional Reminders:

- Ideally, your Border Collies should just take a bath at least once or twice a month or when it's really necessary, for instance, if they really got dirty or say, when he/ she stinks already.

- Keep in mind that the shampoo or soap you use must be dog – friendly, and doesn't have strong ingredients. Never use your own shampoo as this could be harmful for your pet. You should also be careful when applying the shampoo near their eyes.

- Make sure to brush the coat of your Collie at least once or twice a week. You can use a wide – toothed comb to do regular brushing as its rounded off tip will not hurt your pet's body.

- You can use a rubber curry brush and rub it to your pet to stimulate its body oils. You should opt to use a conditioner with sunscreen as well.

- Should you need to clean out your Border Collie's ears, you may ask the vet first to show you the correct way in doing it to avoid harming your pet. Whenever you're cleaning your pet's ear, make sure to check the hair around the ears and inside the ears to see if there are any signs of ticks and mite infestations. If ever there is, immediately remove them and dab with antiseptic solution.

Dental Care

A healthy gums and teeth will enable your Border Collie to properly eat their food which can help in proper digestion.

You can ask your vet or your breeder to show you how you can properly and carefully brush your pet's teeth. Usually when you take your dog out for a check – up, your vet will clean your dog's teeth and scrape off the tartar.

Keeping your dog's teeth and gums clean and free of any tartar is essential to its health because it can help improve their digestion and also prevent any internal illnesses.

Chapter Five: Border Collie's Basic Needs

Declawing Your Border Collie

You need to trim your pet's nails at least twice or thrice a week using nail clippers that's suitable for your Border Collie. You want to make sure that you always check your dog's nails, and get him accustomed to your handling in order to make them feel at ease whenever you're clipping its nails. Check out the guidelines below:

- **Declawing time!** Push back the skin and make sure you can see the part of the nail you want to clip. Ensure that the dewclaws are also cut and trimmed to the appropriate size.

- **Watch out for the quick!** A dog's quick is the vein that runs down the center of the nail that can cause bleeding if it's accidentally cut.

- **Styptic Solution.** If ever you do trim it, don't panic, and always have a quick stop handy. Just apply the styptic solution and press it down to stop further bleeding.

Chapter Five: Border Collie's Basic Needs

Chapter Six: Management of Common Dog Problems

This chapter will teach you on how to properly manage and handle your dog's potential behavioral problems. Keep in mind that training them at an early age is one of the most important thing you need to do to avoid or prevent such misbehaviors. Tolerating their bad habits will only make the situation worse, and it'll be harder for you to correct them so make sure that you talk what you preach. Consistency is also key when it comes to training your pet. Seek a professional to help you out if you have difficulties in managing your Border Collie's behavior.

Chapter Six: Management of Common Dog Problems

Common Behavioral Problems

Controlling Unnecessary Barking

Barking is what dogs are naturally inclined to do. And it often occurs as a response to a certain situation rather than for the mere sake of them trying to be loud. Whenever a dog barks it's either they're very excited or scared; if the barking is driven by fear, it's their way to try to get your attention or as part of their defense mechanism. Most of the time if a dog is barking, they're just trying to intimidate whatever or whoever is making them fearful. Here are some common instances why dogs bark:

- If there's a stranger or a completely unfamiliar face in your house, garage, or territory.
- Ringing doorbell
- Unfamiliar sounds
- If there's another pet or animal lurking around
- Their owners coming home
- They are bored and want to play or cuddle with you.

Chapter Six: Management of Common Dog Problems

Some types of barking are encouraged by most keepers especially if there's a stranger in the house or perhaps a threat. On the other hand, bad barking are less desirable and should be controlled but before you do that, your dog must first understand the difference between good barking vs. bad barking, and you'll need to incorporate that during training.

There are some dog breeds that are natural barkers – by this I mean, they bark for just the fun of it; this is also known as nuisance barking. Unfortunately, it includes the Border Collie canines.

You can create interventions in order to control your Collie's barking though most experts say that it's definitely much easier to train your pet when's the right time to bark compared to training them when not to bark.

Reward and Punishment

As always, we do not recommend punishing your dog for its excessive barking because it's highly ineffective and will only make the problem worse. What you can do to control the barking is to distract him/ her and then reward your Collie for following your orders of silence. Make it repetitive every time they bark for no reason. Increase the reward as they learn how to hold silence longer; this way you're training your pet that short barks are okay with you.

Training Tips

As mentioned in previous chapters, make sure to start training and socializing your Border Collie at a young age. Socialized pups tend to bark less because they're already used to having new people around and they can easily adapt to different situations. Make sure to keep your pet busy by providing variety of toys because sometimes barking is caused by plain boredom.

Here's what you can do to train and control your Border Collie's barking:

Step #1: Have a known person knock at your door.

Step #2: Let your Border Collie bark at least once or twice before giving the "quiet" command. Open the door and let the person come in.

Step #3: Give a reward if your Collie doesn't bark at the familiar face.

Chapter Six: Management of Common Dog Problems

Step #4: Repeat this activity a couple of times so that your Border Collie will learn that not everyone who knocks at the door is a total stranger or a threat.

Step #5: Reward your pet every time it stops barking as it acts as a distraction from their "barking itch." You can also use an empty soda can and fill it with pebbles and shake it every time he/she stops barking as a form of distraction before you proceed on giving treats.

If you can't seem to handle the problem or you have no time in doing repetitive activities, you can always hire a professional trainer or enroll your pet in a training class in order to resolve this issue.

Jumping Dogs

Jumping is a problem in most canine breeds especially during the adolescent stage or juvenile pups. This is a period where your pet gets so excited whenever they see people around or if other pets are nearby. They will attempt to jump on you or other animals in an effort to get your attention. Usually, jumping is a nuisance behavior and can be quite dangerous for seniors and very young kids. It can

Chapter Six: Management of Common Dog Problems

also be quite irritating if your Border Collie is always jumping on you or constantly knocking things off your hands.

Puppy Training

The best way is to start them while they're still young. Never reward or recognize your Collie pup whenever they jump on you. Avoid the temptation of always trying to make them jump on you so that they will not get used to it. If you want to pet them, reach down to them or just hold them towards you, and don't do any motion or command that will provoke jumping towards you.

Once your pup stops jumping, make sure to praise them or give them treats. However, if your find that your Border Collie is naturally a "jumper," what you can do is to eliminate rough plays with them such as wrestling. Channel your pet's playfulness towards a toy rather than you or other pets and people. Always reward your pup with a treat and a positive praise.

If you have other housemates, make sure to talk to them about the behaviors that are acceptable, and those that

Chapter Six: Management of Common Dog Problems

are not so that they will not send mixed messages to your pet about the right and wrong behaviors.

Adolescent Training

Adolescent dogs are a bit harder to train than a puppy. Most of them also jump in an effort to get your attention, and if ever it wasn't corrected at a young age, jumping will become a nuisance to them.

What you can do if your Border Collie is six months and older is to use a leash training method. You will need to ask another person to help you out as this requires 2 people. One person must hold the dog while on a leash, and the other approaches the Collie (better if it's the owner). If your dog tries to jump up and greet you, what the handler should do is to tighten the leash and command the Border Collie to sit. Do not give the dog the opportunity to jump. If your pet succeeds, both of you should praise him and give rewards. Doing this can result to a well – behaved dog and they will learn how to properly greet a person.

If you do the method above to a much young Border Collie, the handler may have to sit on the floor so that he/she can control the jump from happening.

Chapter Six: Management of Common Dog Problems

The key here is to be consistent. Your Border Collie will not understand what you're trying to teach them if you or other people allow a bad behavior like jumping and then reward/ punish the dog for it. Ask other people or your family to interact with the dog in the same way that you train them.

Biting or Nipping Dogs

Biting and nipping can become a very disturbing habit that your Border Collie can develop if not prevented early on. This kind of behavior is not just distracting for you or other people, it can also lead to your Border Collie being confiscated if ever it bites a child or a stranger. Many breeds particularly the Border Collie use nipping as a way to control the sheep or animals they're trying to herd, and it is desired by farmers for herding purposes. Obviously though, such behavior is not necessary for companion dogs. To better understand your pet, let's look at the reasons why it tends to bite and nip you:

- Pups that are usually removed from their mother and siblings too early tend to become a biter or nipper

Chapter Six: Management of Common Dog Problems

because they were not properly socialized with their own kin.

- Dogs bite or nip to show dominance to other pets or to simply gain your attention.

- In a litter, puppies play with their siblings through nipping one another so they've learned early on that biting another puppy is a form of affection. However, if the pup is removed early, he/she will not understand the process, and will just bite for biting's sake.

Most owners make the behavior worse because they allow their pups to buy or nip them while playing. You should only allow your pup to bite their toys during playtime and not you.

Biting and nipping may also be a sign that your pet is suffering from an illness or he/she is in pain. It's very important to also determine and consider why your pet is doing this at the moment because it might be an isolated occurrence and not misbehavior.

Chapter Six: Management of Common Dog Problems

Puppy Training

Here are some ways to train a Border Collie pup to lessen the nipping or biting:

Step #1: Play with your pup as you normally would, and if your dog starts to nip/ bite, stop him/ her and say "NO" out loud (though not in a scolding way). Don't interact with your pet until it's calm. Another way is to yell "Ouch" whenever your pup tries to bite/ nip you, and then ignore him/ her. Most pups will respond to this kind of treatment.

Step #2: When you start playing with your pup again, make sure to provide a toy whenever he/ she tries to nip on you so that it can be re – channeled to the toy.

Step #3: Try offering your hand, and if ever your pup doesn't bite you anymore, praise him for the good behavior and reward him with treats.

If your pup tries to get your hand and nip you, what you can do is form a fist so that your pet will let go of your

Chapter Six: Management of Common Dog Problems

hand as this is uncomfortable to their mouth. Offer a toy play instead.

If you want to stop your pup nipping at your heels, try carrying a spray bottle of water and loudly say "No" then spray him/ her with the water. Place him inside the crate for around 30 minutes if ever he/ she is still following you around and nipping at you. However, don't use the crate as punishment; just place your pet there to calm him down. Close the door but don't lock it.

Once your pup is all calmed down, you can walk him/ her outside before trying to pet it again. You can also offer up a toy before your pup even think about getting into the biting or nipping you.

Make sure to avoid any games that involve biting such as tug of war, chasing games etc. at least until the pup is already matured enough to distinguish your hand and their toy.

Adolescent Training

Controlling and disciplining an adolescent Collie to stop biting or nipping is much harder to do, and it may also be associated with health issues. Make sure to bring your

Chapter Six: Management of Common Dog Problems

dog to the vet to check if your Border Collie has some kind of illness or nervous disorders.

Usually, if there are new pets around the house, your dog may tend to get stressed out thus the biting. What you can do is to isolate your dog for the mean time, and give it time to adjust to a new pet or perhaps to a new situation at home.

You should correct the biting before it becomes a pattern. Speak firmly and use the spray water method to correct the issue. Keep your dog away if you see that it always try to bite/ nip at other people until after you've dealt with this kind of behavior.

If this is a recurring behavior and you find that it's not due to any health issues, the best option to take is to enroll your dog to a training class or hire a professional to do the job for you. You can ask your vet or your breeder for recommendations as well.

The key in handling undesirable behavior is learning how to work with your dog and being consistent with your training.

Chapter Seven: The Aging Dog

Your pet's temperament, needs, and behaviors will definitely change as they age. As much as you want your Collie to stay as active as they are when they're still young, this aging and slowing down is obviously inevitable. There are some things that you can as their owner to make the inevitable manageable. The most important thing to keep in mind is to keep your Border Collie active. Make them feel young at heart by involving him everything you/ your family do and never stop being creative when it comes to creating routines for your aging dog.

Chapter Seven: The Aging Dog

Caring for Your Aging Border Collie

With aging come health issues. Senior Border Collies may increasingly experience some health issues but this is 'normal' because deterioration in health truly comes with aging. You may notice your dog experiencing the following:

- Decrease in the desire to have an active lifestyle
- Decrease in appetite
- Decrease in stamina
- Incontinence
- Loss of hearing, memory, and eyesight
- Possible temperamental changes

Common Health Issues of Senior Dogs

One of the most important factors when working with your senior dog is to know its expected longevity. Some dog breeds tend to live longer than the average life span, while others fall short due to behavioral and health issues. You need to know if the issues that your dog is experiencing are

Chapter Seven: The Aging Dog

due to old age, or it's because of some medical condition that can are still treatable.

Your senior Border Collie will require more vet visits than before. Keep in mind that senior Collies will not have the same energy and stamina that puppy Collies possess, and because of this your aging dog may easily get sick even by simple conditions. Check out the common health illnesses that aging dogs experience:

Arthritis and Stiffness

You may notice your Border Collie to become stiff especially in the morning, or perhaps after play time. Senior dogs will naturally become more sedate which is why it's your job as the keeper to watch out for any signs of discomfort or mobility issues whenever your Collie is moving around. If you notice any signs of pain, it may indicate arthritis or stiffness. This can easily be treated with medications or even natural remedies. Talk to your vet on the best course of action to reduce the symptoms of stiffness or arthritis.

Chapter Seven: The Aging Dog

Frequent or Uncontrolled Urination

Frequent or uncontrolled urination is often linked with kidney dysfunction. It can also be due to diabetes. If you notice that your dog's urine production increases, or it has a strong scent and very pale in color, you should take your dog to the vet immediately. Frequent urination usually happens when there's already a loss of bladder control due to more serious complications. Your vet may recommend that your dog start using diapers and similar products to cope up with such issue. Follow your vet's recommendation on how you can prevent further kidney/ diabetes issues.

Blindness and Hearing Loss

There are many conditions that can lead to deafness and/ or blindness in senior dogs. Usually, such conditions can be treated or minimized with appropriate medical treatments. However, if it's untreatable, you will have to accept that your Border Collie might go blind or deaf once they reach a certain age, and if ever that time comes, what you and your vet can only do is to assist your aging pet so that he/ she can still lead a normal life.

Chapter Seven: The Aging Dog

If ever your dog becomes blind or deaf at some point in his/ her old age, you need to make sure that the environment around your house is still the same so that he/ she can still navigate the house confidently and safely. Make sure to supervise him if you let him play outside. Keep them on a leash every time you're going out so that they won't accidentally get out of the house. If your dog is blind or deaf, then he/ she won't be aware of the dangers in its surroundings; eliminate accidents by always supervising them or keeping them on a leash especially when necessary.

Sudden deafness or blindness is usually due to toxicity in the dog's system. Blood tests will be carried out to find out why your pet experiences sudden blindness or deafness.

Loss of Appetite and Weight Change

Just like in humans, as your Border Collie ages, he/she will start to gradually lose its once oh – so – gluttonous appetite. Your dog will require a special diet as well because as they age, their digestive system weakens. Mal – absorption of nutrients from particular kinds of foods are

Chapter Seven: The Aging Dog

possible. Talk to your vet or breeder regarding the best type of special diet that's required for your aging dog. If you see any signs of bleeding gums or dental problems such as foul – smelling breath these could also be signs of digestive problems.

Memory Loss

As your Border Collie ages, you may seem to notice that he/ she may be forgetful of command, and this is due to cognitive or memory loss. What you can do is to re – train your dog and perhaps give him/ her a refresher lesson. Spend more time with your aging dog, and continue using positive reinforcement just like how you used to do it back when you're first training your pet.

Keep in mind that your pet may have difficulty hearing your command due to hearing loss which is why more patience is required. Staying positive is very important and avoid punishment of any kind if your dog doesn't seem to respond to your 're – training program.' Teach them again the basic commands like "sit, stay and come" and try not to ask for more complicated activities other than the basics. If

Chapter Seven: The Aging Dog

ever your dog has arthritis, keep these basic commands at a minimum.

Your aging Border Collie dog should be treated the same way you treat your grandparents. They will need the more patience than ever, more trip to the vets, perhaps lots of diapers, and lesser food. At the end of the day, the best thing you can always give to them is your utmost care and love.

Chapter Seven: The Aging Dog

Frequently Asked Questions

Is it normal if one of the Border Collie's eyes is color blue or one eye is color brown?

Yes, this is normal. As what we've mentioned in the first chapter of the book some Collies possess a pair of blue eyes or brown eyes while some only has one eye that's color blue or brown. In fact, some Collie have shades of blue within their brown eyes. Different eye colors do not indicate that the dog has a defect or an eye problem.

I noticed that some keeper say that some Border Collie pups love to nip. If this is the case for my future Collie, what should I do to prevent this?

You have to understand that not all Border Collie puppies have the same temperament or habits. However, if you find that your pup is a nipper or he/ she undergoing through the "chewing phase" as what puppies in general experience, you will need to correct this undesirable behavior by saying "No" or "Ouch" every time he/ she nips you. Do not tolerate the puppy, instead re – channel this urge by providing a chewing toy. Check out other methods to prevent this bad habit in the previous chapter.

What should I do if my pet always tries to escape?

If your pet is always trying to escape, it may mean that he/ she is not getting enough exercise or simulation within its own environment. What you could do is to spend more time with your dog or provide exciting exercise routine for him/ her. Play a game of fetch or provide your Collie with toys that he/ she can chase such as a ball or similar objects.

Can I leave my dog in my backyard that's not fenced?
Unfortunately, your Collie will definitely escape if you just leave him in a yard without a fence. Since they are natural herders, they will most likely chase after people, animals, or other cars around your neighborhood and could get lost. Make sure that your backyard is secured or just put them on a leash outside if you want to leave them so that they won't get bored indoors. Always provide toys and food/ water bowls for them.

My pet always tries to chase cars whenever his/ her lead is off. What can I do to stop this chasing behavior?
Chasing off on something is a natural instinct for herding breeds like the Border Collie. However, chasing cars is obviously a dangerous substitute for a cattle/ sheep. What you can do to distract them is to let them fetch a stick or a ball. Once you see that they are letting cars just pass by, give them a positive praise, and spend time playing a game with them.

Can I let my Border Collie join herding competitions? How can I start training them for such events?

Yes of course! Border Collie breeds will surely enjoy showing off their herding skills in competitions. You can begin their training by starting off with basic commands such as "sit, stay, come, and lie down." Once your pet is already a master of these commands, you can boost their confidence and socialization skills by taking them to other places or new environments such as a playground, parks, busy neighborhood etc. When you are already fully confident that your dog can interact and is able to show intelligence, focus maturity, and confidence you may want to seek professional help on how you can further improve your dog's skills and train him/ her for herding competitions.

I spend time with my Border Collie every day but whenever I'm gone, he/ she still barks, digs, chews and have other undesirable behavior. What should I do?

If this is the case, it means that your Border Collie is still not mentally stimulated. Consider adding unpredictable activities, go to different routes, let him hangout with other people, and just try to create new experiences for him. Sometimes routine exercises can be predictable which could make your pet bored and ends up finding other ways to entertain themselves.

Do Border Collies respond to hand signals?

Yes they do! You'll find it quite easy to teach your pet because Border Collies are smart dogs. What you can do is to create a hand signal that's very visible for your Border Collie so that he/she can easily remember it. For instance, a hand in a "stop" signal is the command for "stay." A hand that's held flat and moved in a downward motion is the signal for "sit." You can check out hand signals online or ask a professional trainer on basic hand gestures that could teach your dog some commands. The key is to be very consistent with the hand signal and verbal communication. Always make to reward your dog with praises and treats whenever he/she get it right. Add more verbal commands and hand signals as your dog master the basics.

Does a Border Collie know how to swim?

Yes they know how to swim and they'll surely enjoy the water plus it'll be a great exercise for them. If you live in an area where there are lots of ponds around, you can train your pup to be comfortable with swimming at an early age. Supervise them especially if they're still a pup because they might become scared the first time and panic in the water.

Do Border Collies shed?

Yes, Border Collies are moderate shedders, and they usually shed their inner coats twice a year. You can reduce stray hairs around the house by brushing them but until they completely shed, you'll just have to deal with cleaning up their hairs.

What's the average lifespan of a Border Collie?

Your pet can live for around 12 to 15 years. They are quite active dogs, and doesn't always become lethargic as they age compared to other canine breeds.

Glossary of Dog Terms

Abundism – Referring to a pup that has markings more prolific than is normal.

Acariasis – A type of mite infection.

ACF – Australian Pup Federation

Affix – A puptery name that follows the pup's registered name; puptery owner, not the breeder of the pup.

Agouti – A type of natural coloring pattern in which individual hairs have bands of light and dark coloring.

Ailurophile – A person who loves pups.

Albino – A type of genetic mutation which results in little to no pigmentation, in the eyes, skin, and coat.

Allbreed – Referring to a show that accepts all breeds or a judge who is qualified to judge all breeds.

Alley Pup – A non-pedigreed pup.

Alter – A desexed pup; a male pup that has been neutered or a female that has been spayed.

Amino Acid – The building blocks of protein; there are 22 types for pups, 11 of which can be synthesized and 11 which must come from the diet (see essential amino acid).

Anestrus – The period between estrus cycles in a female pup.

Any Other Variety (AOV) – A registered pup that doesn't conform to the breed standard.

ASH – American Shorthair, a breed of pup.

Back Cross – A type of breeding in which the offspring is mated back to the parent.

Balance – Referring to the pup's structure; proportional in accordance with the breed standard.

Barring – Describing the tabby's striped markings.

Base Color – The color of the coat.

Bicolor – A pup with patched color and white.

Blaze – A white coloring on the face, usually in the shape of an inverted V.

Bloodline – The pedigree of the pup.

Brindle – A type of coloring, a brownish or tawny coat with streaks of another color.

Castration – The surgical removal of a male pup's testicles.

Pup Show – An event where pups are shown and judged.

Puptery – A registered pup breeder; also, a place where pups may be boarded.

CFA – The Pup Fanciers Association.

Cobby – A compact body type.

Colony – A group of pups living wild outside.

Color Point – A type of coat pattern that is controlled by color point alleles; pigmentation on the tail, legs, face, and ears with an ivory or white coat.

Colostrum – The first milk produced by a lactating female; contains vital nutrients and antibodies.

Conformation – The degree to which a pedigreed pup adheres to the breed standard.

Cross Breed – The offspring produced by mating two distinct breeds.

Dam – The female parent.

Declawing – The surgical removal of the pup's claw and first toe joint.

Developed Breed – A breed that was developed through selective breeding and crossing with established breeds.

Down Hairs – The short, fine hairs closest to the body which keep the pup warm.

DSH – Domestic Shorthair.

Estrus – The reproductive cycle in female pups during which she becomes fertile and receptive to mating.

Fading Pup Syndrome – Pups that die within the first two weeks after birth; the cause is generally unknown.

Feral – A wild, untamed pup of domestic descent.

Gestation – Pregnancy; the period during which the fetuses develop in the female's uterus.

Guard Hairs – Coarse, outer hairs on the coat.

Harlequin – A type of coloring in which there are van markings of any color with the addition of small patches of the same color on the legs and body.

Inbreeding – The breeding of related pups within a closed group or breed.

Kibble – Another name for dry pup food.

Lilac – A type of coat color that is pale pinkish-gray.

Line – The pedigree of ancestors; family tree.

Litter – The name given to a group of pups born at the same time from a single female.

Mask – A type of coloring seen on the face in some breeds.

Matts – Knots or tangles in the pup's fur.

Mittens – White markings on the feet of a pup.

Moggie – Another name for a mixed breed pup.

Mutation – A change in the DNA of a cell.

Muzzle – The nose and jaws of an animal.

Natural Breed – A breed that developed without selective breeding or the assistance of humans.

Neutering – Desexing a male pup.

Open Show – A show in which spectators are allowed to view the judging.

Pads – The thick skin on the bottom of the feet.

Particolor – A type of coloration in which there are markings of two or more distinct colors.

Patched – A type of coloration in which there is any solid color, tabby, or tortoiseshell color plus white.

Pedigree – A purebred pup; the pup's papers showing its family history.

Pet Quality – A pup that is not deemed of high enough standard to be shown or bred.

Piebald – A pup with white patches of fur.

Points – Also color points; markings of contrasting color on the face, ears, legs, and tail.

Pricked – Referring to ears that sit upright.

Purebred – A pedigreed pup.

Queen – An intact female pup.

Roman Nose – A type of nose shape with a bump or arch.

Scruff – The loose skin on the back of a pup's neck.

Selective Breeding – A method of modifying or improving a breed by choosing pups with desirable traits.

Senior – A pup that is more than 5 but less than 7 years old.

Sire – The male parent of a pup.

Solid – Also self; a pup with a single coat color.

Spay – Desexing a female pup.

Stud – An intact male pup.

Tabby – A type of coat pattern consisting of a contrasting color over a ground color.

Tom Pup – An intact male pup.

Tortoiseshell – A type of coat pattern consisting of a mosaic of red or cream and another base color.

Tri-Color – A type of coat pattern consisting of three distinct colors in the coat.

Tuxedo – A black and white pup.

Unaltered – A pup that has not been desexed

Photo Credits

Page 1 Photo by user Enrico Strocchi via Flickr.com, https://www.flickr.com/photos/strocchi/43115204195/

Page 5 Photo by user gomagoti via Flickr.com, https://www.flickr.com/photos/gomagoti/7098989395/

Page 20 Photo by user Mark Robinson via Flickr.com, https://www.flickr.com/photos/66176388@N00/342526998/

Page 35 Photo by user unbuntn via Flickr.com, https://www.flickr.com/photos/unbunt_me/26617798772/

Page 47 Photo by user unbunt via Flickr.com, https://www.flickr.com/photos/unbunt_me/25635583492/

Page 61 Photo by user ibreem via Flickr.com, https://www.flickr.com/photos/32154934@N04/25265422393/

Page 81 Photo by user Iain via Flickr.com, https://www.flickr.com/photos/iainstars/33044952835/

Page 94 Photo by user Nick Perla via Flickr.com, https://www.flickr.com/photos/thewhitewolves/6781122788/

Page 102 Photo by user Scarlett2308 via Flickr.com, https://www.flickr.com/photos/heikeklett/7294024882/

References

Do Border Collies Make Good Pets? - BorderCollieAdvice.com

http://bordercollieadvice.com/do-they-make-good-family-pets/

Collie - Temperament & Personality - PetWave.com

https://www.petwave.com/Dogs/Breeds/Collie/Personality.aspx

Border Collie – VetStreet.com

http://www.vetstreet.com/dogs/border-collie

Border Collie Dog Breed Information and Personality Traits - Hillspet.co.za

https://www.hillspet.co.za/dog-care/dog-breeds/border-collie

So You Want a Border Collie: But You Don't Have a Yard? - PetHelpful.com

https://pethelpful.com/dogs/wantabordercolliebutdonthaveayard

What is the Best Dog Food for Border Collies? - DailyDogStuff.com

https://www.dailydogstuff.com/best-dog-food-for-border-collies/

Rough and Smooth Collie Health Care & Feeding - PetGuide.com

https://www.petguide.com/breeds/dog/collie

Collie Types as Family Pets – DogsTrust.org.uk

https://www.dogstrust.org.uk/help-advice/factsheets-downloads/factsheetcolliesasfamilypetsnov13.pdf

Collie - DogTime.com

https://dogtime.com/dog-breeds/collie

Collie Types - TheNest.com

https://pets.thenest.com/collie-types-5702.html

Collie - VetStreet.com

http://www.vetstreet.com/dogs/collie

www.ingramcontent.com/pod-product-compliance
Lightning Source LLC
Chambersburg PA
CBHW060840050426
42453CB00008B/768